CLASSROOM TAPESTRY

WEAVING the HEARTS, SOULS, and MINDS of STUDENTS

CLASSROOM TAPESTRY

WEAVING the HEARTS, SOULS, and MINDS of STUDENTS

Lori DeJong

REDEMPTION
PRESS
EXPRESS

ISBN 13: 978-1-68314-931-6

Library of Congress Catalog Card Number: 2024909748

PREFACE

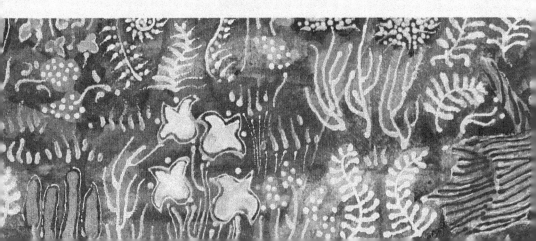

GOD'S DIVINE GIFT

GOD'S DIVINE GIFT

The divine gift of language is given to all humans by God's common grace. It is the vehicle that allows us to communicate information and form relationships. The tools used in this act of communication are listening, speaking, reading, and writing.

The first two, listening and speaking, are present at birth in the form of crying. Listening is receptive, allowing the newborn to receive communication. Speaking is generative, allowing the newborn to communicate. Every parent can attest to a baby's effectiveness at these skills.

The moment of birth is a wonderful glimpse of God's wisdom. Notice the physical closeness necessary for both listening and speaking. A baby needs to be held and soothed with voice, touch, and eye contact. A baby cannot write out or text his desire for milk or attention. Likewise, you cannot text a soothing message to a baby.

I have friends who are "cuddlers" at a local hospital. Their job is to hold and soothe these newborns with touch, voice, and eye contact. Their physical presence is literally lifesaving in the case of some of these premature babies who are born addicted to drugs.

The next tools, reading and writing, are acquired as the child matures and progresses toward literacy. As literacy develops, the receptive, at-birth skill of listening widens into the receptive literacy skill of reading. Likewise, the generative at-birth ability to speak (cry, scream, whimper, and whine) widens into the generative literary skill of writing.

Literacy, the ability to understand that letter symbols (the alphabet) are related to sounds (phonics), is acquired early on. Again, God's wisdom allows for the skill to enlarge as the child grows and matures, encouraging independence.

Reading and writing transcend space and time. There may be a great range of distance, time, and autonomy between the reader and the writer. The most wonderful example of this is the Bible. Through God's Word, He communicates to us how to live in this imperfect world: " Love the Lord your God with all your heart and with all your soul and with all your mind. This is the first and greatest commandment. And the second is like it: Love your neighbor as yourself" (Matthew 22: 37-39). It also tells us how to receive eternal salvation with Him and the way to eternity with Him: "For God so loved the world that he gave his one and only Son, that whoever believes in him shall not perish but have eternal life" (John 3:16).

Indeed, God's divine gift!

INTRODUCTION

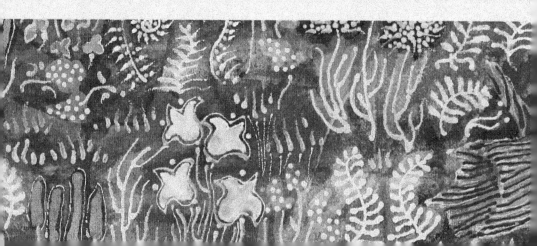

INTRODUCTION

When I was asked what I did for a living, my response often received one of two reactions: either a hand on my shoulder with a look that said, "I'm sorry," or a step back with a look that said, "What is wrong with you?"

Indeed, my answer deserved both responses. You see, I was a junior high school teacher. Yes, junior high or middle school, as it is more commonly referred to now. It is a very easy age group to teach. I mean, at what other age are you going to have students who know everything? They're at that point in their journey where they have all the answers!

As you read through this collection of poetry and writing in the students' own voices, you will see they do indeed have more answers than we give them credit for.

It all started with an ordinary brown cardboard box. There was nothing special about it. A cube: twelve by twelve by twelve. The kind you can buy in any moving-supply store. For many years, it rested mostly unnoticed on a shelf in a cabinet in the far back corner of my seventh-and-eighth-grade language arts classroom. Whenever I opened the cabinet, I saw it but never gave it much thought. I just remembered that it contained some of the writing my students had produced a few years back.

When I was given a new school assignment, the box came with me, where it again cozied down on another shelf in another cabinet in the back corner of another classroom. For three years it remained there, untouched, until that joyous day when I cleaned out my classroom and closed the door for the last time. As I handed my keys to the secretary in the front office, it hit me … I was retired! YAY!

Retirement was great! Traveling in our RV, spoiling our grandkids, and participating in various church ministries occupied my time. Then one afternoon about five years later, I was sitting in my sunny home office admiring the pictures of my grandkids spread across the shelves that surrounded me. A faint memory floated to the top of my thoughts. The memory moved into curiosity, which prompted me to get out of my chair and walk out to the garage.

I retrieved the box and saw the pile of papers I put there over eighteen years ago. I pulled out a folder marked "Student Poetry". Inside were copies of poems that my students had written in 2001.

I had taught a poetry unit, and the end-of-the-unit assignment was a scrapbook of poetry written by the students, including various types of poetry we had studied: haiku, autobiographical, freestyle, diamante, etc. After grading their scrapbooks, I made copies of them and returned the originals to the students, promising myself that I would take time to enjoy them later. Well, another lesson, more grading, report cards, and a million other things kept me from getting back to rereading them.

Little did I know that opening that box was the beginning of a new journey!

As I read and reflected on the poems, I realized the greatest treasure of my teaching was my memories. These memories were the blessings I received from participating in the lives of so many young people who were at a crossroads in their lives.

This realization expressed itself perfectly in the form of a poem a thirteen-year-old boy had written in his poetry scrapbook:

Memories

Lost or found, memories live on
Sometimes forgotten
Sometimes remembered
Do with them what you wish
For they are yours to possess

Whether you cherish them or hate them
They are born from your experience
They are not to be taken for granted
Lost or found, memories live on

Amazing! The irony that a student's writing under my tutelage at the beginning of his life's journey would now give me direction and focus at this point in my life's journey!

That is what this book is about: the two-way street of lessons learned, those I taught to my students and those my students taught me. It is a tapestry of sparkling strands of student poetry, yarn bits of priceless gifts, interlaced stories from the classroom, and cords of lessons and teaching strategies that empowered students to become independent learners. This tapestry is made up of the hearts, souls, and minds of my students and, yes, also of mine!

Are you ready to listen to the voices that came from the box?

Warning … have your handkerchief ready. You will be crying tears of sadness and joy, often at the same time.

GLITTERING
STRANDS
OF

STUDENT POETRY

GLITTERING STRANDS OF STUDENT POETRY

1. **PARENT DESERTION**
   Students share the pain of having been deserted by a parent.

2. **GIRLS AND BOYS**
   Girls and boys muse about the strange behaviors of the opposite sex while also confessing a strong interest in them.

3. **SPORTS**
   The highs and lows of being involved in sports.

4. **NATURE**
   From the sweet smell of flowers to the beauty of a butterfly, these poems capture the magic and magnitude of nature and the outdoors.

5. **FOOD**
   An interesting perspective on food from a teen's point of view.

6. **LOST LOVE**
   Vignettes of lost loves.

7. **LIFE'S UNANSWERED QUESTIONS**
   From "being alone in this nightmare" to "our painful 9/11 memories will never go away," these poems wonder and ponder, Why?

8. **FRIENDSHIP**
   The joy and sadness of friendship.

9. **WISDOM FROM THE MOUTH OF BABES**
   Life from the perspective of a thirteen-year-old.

Warning! Have your handkerchief nearby!

PARENT
DESERTION

Why?

Why don't you love me?
Why don't you hug me?
Why don't you ever lie down?

Why didn't I miss you?
Why didn't I tell you?
Why didn't I ever say
I love you?
Because you were never around!

—Stephanie B.

Mom

Mom...why?
Why aren't you here for me?
Why don't you care for me?
Why don't you ever come around?

Why don't you kiss me?
Why don't you miss me?
Why don't you ever come around?

Why don't you hug me?
Why don't you love me?
Why don't you ever come around?

Again and again...
I remind myself...
You never even said good-bye!!!
Mom...why?

Dad

Dad...thanks!
You are here for me!
You care for me!
You are always around!

You kiss me!
You miss me!
You are always around!

You hug me!
You love me!
You are always around!

Again and again...
I remind myself...
How lucky I am to have you!
Dad...thanks! I love you!!!

—Kayla B.

I love you, I love you
I really do
But you must understand, Mommy
I love Daddy, too.

—Rachel D.

The Forgiving Blue Sea

You weren't there for me
When I needed you.
You always said
You had something to do.
I saw you do this.
I saw you do that.
And you never once stopped
To give me a pat on the back.
And now that I
Am older and stronger
I realize it was you
Who did it all wrong.
But with a year older
Comes another year wiser
And with many more years
My eyes open wider.
So if you have something
You want to say to me
Just toss it into
The forgiving blue sea.

—Alice S.

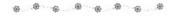

My Mother

I remember her face
But she left with no trace
I think sometimes she's next to me
But how can she be?

I remember her touch
But not all that much
I think I see her in my dreams
But who could she be?

I remember my father told me
That she used to be there
But I wonder how she can be
My Mother!

—Rachel D.

How Come?

How come you left my mommy?
How come you left me, Daddy?
How come I love you?
How come you don't love me?

How come you never took care of me?
How come you only came when I was three?
How come you never bought me a toy, maybe a ball?
How come you never called?

How come you married another woman?
How come you had more children?
How come you weren't there for me?
How come you aren't here now?

How come you never come to see me?
How come I don't even know where you live?
How come I love you, Daddy?
How come you don't love me?

—Cynthia M.

Is There a Reason?

Is there a reason
You act like you aren't there?
Is there a reason
You act like you don't care?

Is there a reason?
Please Daddy, I need to know.
Is she the reason?
The woman you know?

—Alice S.

GIRLS AND BOYS

Boys

Pigs, Jerks, Pervs
Nerds, Dorks, Stupid Retards
Rhinoceros Butts
Lazy, Couch Potatoes
Conniving, Pimple Punks
Puke Faces, Maggots
Geeks, Cheaters,
Players, Snobs
Irresponsible, Disgusting Dogs
I LOVE THEM!!!

—Katie T.

Boys

What's up with boys?
Why are they so hot...and not!
Why do I love them?

—Katie T.

G. I. R. L. S.

G is for girls who giggle and give
I is for inner beauty from girls who know how to live
R is for ridiculously caring for me all the time
L is for nice legs and letting me ride on your bike pegs
S is for sexy and silly and for not cheating on me with Billy.

—Gus S.

My Perfect Girl

Who will be my perfect girl?
What will she look like?

I saw this girl with perfect legs
She was staring at me, standing still
But I had to walk away after she smiled at me
And I saw this honey's grill.

I walked down the street and saw another
This girl had curves that could
Only be ridden by a hummer
But since she was blond I was afraid she was dumber.

I saw another girl who I thought I saw before
I walked up to her not knowing what was in store
As she came up to me
She slapped me and I hit the floor.

The last girl I saw was perfect in every way
I was anxious to hear what she had to say
She came to talk to me wearing all baby blue
The only thing wrong was her nasty attitude.

Now I know what my perfect girl will be like
She doesn't need to have a big booty
I figured out that my perfect girl
Will have inner beauty.

—Gus S.

Girls

Some are blond and some have curls
But most of them just want
Diamonds and pearls.

Some are sad and some are happy
But they never even know
That their hair looks sappy.

Some are fine like angels that fly
But just want to go out with you
To get back at another guy.

Girls, Girls, Girls, I'll never understand you
But I know I would go crazy
If the world never had you!

—Gus S.

SPORTS

Game Day

I wake up at 6 A.M.
Even though the game doesn't start until 5 P.M.
I take a long hot shower
Then a long cold bath
I put all my gear on
Except my helmet and pads.

It's now 9 A.M.
I can't stand waiting, so I go stretch out
I come back in and it's only 10 A.M.
Tensions are high and I'm getting very excited
I try everything to release the tension –
Push-ups, sit-ups, punching bag and run.

The tension goes away, but returns even worse
It is now 1 P.M., two hours 'til I leave
Somehow I must stay calm
From the moment I set foot on the football field
I feel that I am home.

You're about to start the game of your life
It's do or die, win or cry
When the game is over, there will be tears
Will they be tears of victory or tears of defeat?

—Stephen C.

Football

On the fifty-yard line it all begins
Between his legs the center snaps the ball
Behind him waits the quarterback
Into waiting hands the pigskin lands
Over their heads the leather missile flies
Toward the eager grasp of the running back
Across the goal line he slides...
TOUCHDOWN!

—Franz L.

Sports

Some sports are tough
Some sports are rough
Some sports make you hurt
Some even make you eat dirt
Some sports are easy
Some are just cheesy
But they're all extremely fun!!!

—Stephen C.

You Can Keep Baseball

Baseball's the sport everyone loves
With a bat in your hand
And a ball in your glove
Baseball is surely a sport from above.

After your turn, when you're playing ball
It goes through the window
And into the hall
Baseball's an expensive sport above all.

After spending the day out there on the lawn
Knowing you gave it your all
Your all is gone
And exhaustion quickly comes in.

Now you can play baseball
And that's OK
But I'll take football
Any old day!

—Stephen C.

NATURE

Flowers

Flowers are like love
In all kinds of ways
They grow and then die
Neither one stays

—**Shawna S.**

Nature

Unpredictable
Full of raging liveliness
Natural beauty

—**Shawna S.**

Aquatic Beauty

The waterfall stands
In great majestic beauty
For all to marvel

—**Ryndie A.**

B LUE

*Blue is for that distant ocean
going on forever
Blue is for the beautiful skies
ending never
Blue is for that sparkle in your
beautiful eyes
Blue is what makes that lovely
rainbow rise.*

—Ryndie A.

Cool, blustery days

*Leaves blowing down the gutter
Fall has befallen*

—Franz L.

Butterflies

Butterflies flutter around me
On wings made of silk and gold
From flower to flower they live so free
Since the days of old

Butterflies landing right on my nose
On my cheeks and in my hair
Landing on a nearby rose
They really seem to care

I dance around the garden
As the butterflies come close
I wonder what they're thinking
No one really knows

Then I hear my mother calling
Calling for me to come in
I tell the butterflies goodbye
Until we dance again

—Ryndie A.

Birds

Birds soar through the air
On wings with many feathers
How elevating!

—Cassie P.

Autumn

A sound of crisp leaves rustling in the trees
A leaf falls in the blowing wind
The lush and bight colors of autumn leave
Red, Yellow, Orange, Brown.

A chill wind blows – a penetrating wind
The feeling of cold on my face
Meandering clouds wander in the sky
Illuminated by the moon and stars so high.

A cloud drifts in front of the golden moon
Distorting its brilliant appearance
The cloud slowly rolls into the distance
I see the man in the moon without interference.

A star can be seen in the dark black night
As it shoots on through the night
Hold the star in your hands, close your eyes
Make a wish then let it go again.

—Cassie P.

Camping

Under the pines with the smell of evergreen
Feeling the wind that blows my hair in my face.
Beside the warmth of the dancing orange flames
Under the moon and the stars shining bright.
Surrounded by mountains
My comfort place.

—Cassie P.

Leaves

Falling by my window
Like the snow that's soon to come
They whisper as the winds blow by
And rustle as I run

They tell me that it's colder now
That winter's coming soon
They tell me that the sun is gone
As I lay inside my room

I listen as they call for me
Falling yellow, brown, and red
They whisper through my window
As I lay inside my bed

I wish that I could follow them
As they travel on their way
Soaring through the air, so lovely and so free
Falling by my window
The leaves – they call to me.

—Cassie P.

Almond Blossoms

Like flakes of snow they swirl around me
Drifting in the air
Their sweet fragrance surrounds me
Filling me with joy as I stand there.

White and soft they gently fall
In their quiet perfect grace
I dance around as I listen to their call
While they fall sweetly on my face.

As I fill myself with power
I let myself be truly free
And dance within the cleansing shower
Of almond blossoms falling on me.

—Ryndie A.

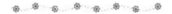

FOOD

Search

Throughout the country
Around the town
Somewhere, surely, it will be found...
Inside the houses
Upon the streets
Soon I shall find what now I seek
Far have I come
Near does it lie
Yes! I've found it!
My chocolate cream pie!

—*Tanner E.*

BOVINE

B is for BIG, what else could I say?
O is for OATS, they chew all day
V is for VERY, as in very boring
I is for IVORY, like milk when it's pouring
N is for NEUTRAL, they're that way at heart.

—*Tanner E.*

Parve

What is parve?
I honestly don't know.
I think this is a good thing.

—Tanner E.

Beast of Evil

I was thoughtless
I knew that
I thought as I passed
Another sizzling, bubbling vat.
It was everywhere now
The plop, goosh and plack
Every new sight made
Me want to go back.

I thought of alternatives
Like selling the house...
Though I'd pity the new owners
When they found out.
I thought to myself then
As I neared the fridge door
How did this happen?
Was my mem'ry so poor?

Now the whole species
Had come alive

And I couldn't believe it
It had actually thrived.
This organic mess
Began to take me in
And I felt a great appendage
Wrap around my skin

"It's all over now..."
I thought to myself
"Now it's going to get me..."
I was now engulfed.
It was truly my fault;
It had gotten out of hand
Now I'm suffering the wrath
OF OLD FORGOTTEN
SPAM

—Tanner E .

Just Deep Fry It

Mushrooms, Potatoes
Salami, Tomatoes
It really doesn't matter what it is.
Meat, Cheese
Chocolate, Peas
Just put it in and make it sizzle
Butter, Toast
Broccoli, Roast
Anything will do, it's really up to you!
JUST DEEP FRY IT

—Tanner E.

Don't ask!!!

"What's for dinner?" I asked my mom.
"Why that's a good idea, little Tom!"
So that night we had "what's"
And to eat that meal, you had to have guts...

—Tanner E.

School Lunch

School lunch
Brown and mushy
Oozing poisonously
Watch out! It looks like it's breathing!
Nasty

—Tanner E.

LOST LOVE

Love

It breaks one's heart to see love die
And then to see the hurt ones cry
Why does this have to happen?
Why can't love just stay alive
And hearts remain unbroken?

—Annie W.

If Only

Beautiful and sweet
Every time I see you I feel like I'm
Falling
Falling
Down a mysterious waterfall
A waterfall that never ends
If only you loved me back...

—Carmen M.

Why?

All my friends ask about you
What should I do?
I tell them things that are not true
But all the lies – they aren't enough
Because the truth about you is very tough
I try every night not to cry
Why did you leave me?
Why did you die?

—Annie W.

Into My Heart

Into my heart
Like a dagger of fire.
Over and apart
It will never tire.

Within my soul
A feeling so new
I'm out in the world
That is now without you.

—Alice S.

The Wait

As he waited outside
Through that gruesome long wait
He began to realize
It might be too late.

As he waited outside
His teeth began to chatter
When he remembered that moment
He saw the glass shatter.

As he waited outside
He prayed like he should
And when the doctor came out
He said, "I did what I could".

As he waited outside
He asked himself "why"
How could this happen?
How could she die?

—Robert M.

I Loved You So Much

I loved you so much
But you let me down
You made me sad
You gave me a frown.

I loved you so much
Then you walked out the door
That's when it happened
When I hit the floor.

I see a bright light now
Way up ahead
That's when I knew
The sad life I had lead.

I'm in heaven now
I knew it was bad
To hurt myself so much
So sad...So sad...

—Gus. S

Why Did You Do It?

Why did you do it
Why did you go
It hurt so bad
Like the chill of snow.

Why did you do it
I saw you there
Kissing that boy
With the silky, black hair.

Why did you do it
I thought you were true
Clearly, I didn't know
I didn't have a clue.

—Gus S.

Why?

Why do things happen?
Things we can't explain
That you wish would just go away
Why does it have to be her?
She's the one I love and I trust
Why can't you leave her alone?
For she is my grandmother
And I want her to stay.

—Rachel D.

Lost

I could search the world until the end
Looking for you again and again
In my dreams you sometimes appear
But when I wake you disappear.

Nearer my heart wants to draw unto you
Further my mind tries to undo the truth
Tick-Tock ... Tick-Tock ... how the clock does keep time
But the memories I have of you will always be mine.

—Andrew R.

Love

What is love?
Love is passion, but breathless
Love can be soft and gentle as a dove.
It's as if you can't live
One day without
If only I know love.

—Shawna S.

Abortion

The day I found out it was true
I didn't know what I should do
Who should I tell or talk to?

This baby was going to be my own
Am I going to be a good mother?
Will my boyfriend and I stay with each other?

What will life be like with this new addition?
Will I have to drop out of school
And miss my graduation?

Should I let this kid ruin my life?
Or just say the word
That will end my fright.

"yes" "no" to the knife ???

—Katie T.

Love

Love is like a star
High up in the sky
The star will never fall
until love dies.

—Stephanie B.

I Remember

I remember yesterday, the walk in the park
The day you said to me, "I'll give you my heart"
Yesterday is gone and now it's today.
I look up and see you with another dumb guy.
I hope he plays you, like you played me
Then you can see, how much trouble you caused me.
With all that trouble and all that pain
I wonder if I'll ever again be sane.

That was then, this is now
That was heaven, this is hell.
So now that you see how hard I fell
I hope you will stop with all the killing.
So please don't let this happen again
Or I might just jump and put all this to an end.
Maybe I will, maybe I won't
But please don't play people like they're a joke.

—Tony T.

I...Don't...Care

I loved you then, I love you now
And then you come and turn my life upside down.
Here I sit, here I lay
Waiting for your call just one more day.
But you never call,
You never talk
You make me feel like a boat
In a lonely dock,
Now I can see that you don't care
Neither do I,
I...just...don't...care.

—Tony T.

LIFE'S UNANSWERED QUESTIONS

Love

Love, love, love
It's all I hear
But, I don't want to love
I don't want to shed a tear

—Robert M.

Alone

I am alone in this nightmare
No one to hold me, no one to care
No one to talk to, no one to share
Please hold me someone
Please someone care.

—Robert M.

Afraid

I'm afraid to show my true feelings
About what I believe
How will people act? What will they think?
But I know this is right for me
And yet I doubt that I am strong enough
To survive the threats and dirty looks they may send
I learn and believe in secret
In fear that I will be found
And shunned by family and friends
Thrown upon the ground.
I don't know if I will make it
But I know I have to try
For if I don't, I will regret it
Until the day I die.

—Andrew R.

Impressions

Impressions are based in all the wrong things
People are judged by the color of their skin
Some judge others by the clothes that they wear
While others judge people by the style of their hair

But these things are not what people should be judged by
To get to know someone you must look eye to eye
Get to know them yourself
Don't listen to what others say
I hope you'll use this as a guide
If you do you'll have many friends at your side.

—Gus S.

The End

It all begins at the end
Death brings forth life
Life ends for more life
Friendships end
Ball games end
Love ends
Suddenly

—Stephanie B.

Dreams

Why do we have dreams?
What do they do?
How do dreams help us?
Without them we'd never know
If dreams really do come true!

—Stephanie B.

Love Is Like an Ocean

Love is like an ocean
Full of emotion
They churn this way and that way
But never in slow motion

Why can't this ocean
Be soothing like potion?
I need a notion
How do I stop this locomotion?

—Stephanie B.

People

Why do people laugh?
Why do people cry?
Why do people whine
every second of their life?
Why don't people realize
What they've already got?
All they worry about is money
And what will be bought.

—Stephanie B.

Love Hurts

Why does love hurt
Like an arrow through your heart?
Why can't love enlighten
Like a flashlight in the dark?

—Stephanie B.

War and Peace

War
Terrible, Unforgiving
Hating, Killing, Ending
Fear, Pain, Beliefs, Ideals
Loving, Living, Beginning
Forgiving, Wonderful
Peace

—Nick T.

Who Do They Think They Are?

Why must my family suffer this terror?
Why must innocent children and women die?
Why do they hate us?
Why must they shoot anyone who walks outside?
How much terror can they possibly do
To make someone commit suicide
Why did they pick us?
Why are they trying to take over our land?
Who are they to give us a curfew?
Who are they to be shooting at children?
Who are they to shoot at teenagers with rocks?
Who are they to make checkpoints in our land?
Who are they to knock over our houses?
Who are they to slap and kick teenagers?
Who are they to kill anyone who stands by a window?
Who are they to take pictures of innocent lives that they've killed?
Who are they to drive tanks all over our towns?
Who are they to kill 30 Palestinians after we injure only 7 of them in a
car bomb?
Who are they to embarrass my country, my family, and me?
Who do they think they are?

—Gus S.

9/11 Attacks

Those people were so wrong
They killed us all.
We lost so many people from this tragic fall.
When those towers came down we cried for days
No one from then on had a smile on their face.

I wish this never happened
It hurt us all
But there's nothing I can do because I'm so small
But my promise to you is that I will pray
For the people and all that happened on that terrible day.

We know that our painful 9/11 memories will never go away.

—Kayla B.

FRIENDSHIP

The Rainbow of Friendship

Red is for lovable
Yellow is for happiness
Blue is for thoughtful
Orange is for trustful
Purple is for comfort
Green is for generosity
These are the colors of the rainbow
When I put them all together
I've got a friend like you.

—Shawna S.

Friends Forever...

Forever we will always be
Right up to the very end
Instead you turned your back on me
Even though we were the best of friends
Nothing is going to be the same
Dealing with all the pain and memories
So for now, FOREVER has come to an end.

—Shawna S.

My Friend

Call me tomorrow to say hello
Or come to me by the weeping willow
Today I think I'll play by the lake
And maybe a sand castle I'll make
Yesterday I flew my kite high, really high
I lost sight of it beyond the clouds in the sky
But tomorrow, my friend, I'll play with you
Or today come join me in everything I do.

—Andrew R.

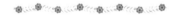

WISDOM FROM THE MOUTH OF BABES

Bring Out Your Smile

Smiles are contagious, on and on they go
Where they stop nobody knows
Smiles are contagious

They make you feel special inside
I try to bring out the ones that hide
Smiles are contagious

On and on and on they go
I'm so glad everyone has
A special smile to show.

—Kayla B.

Colors

Blue is the color of the sky
Yellow is the color of the sun
Blue is the color of the bird that flies
So high...so high...so high...
Colors are feelings and what people become
Colors make up the world around us
They make everything so fun

—Alice S.

Love is Happiness

Some people think money is what life's all about
But they are truly wrong
For people who have no love in their life
Wish for love all day long.

Everyone needs someone to talk to
Just to get thoughts out of their head
Without someone to share and someone to love
You'll be sad and lonely at night in bed.

Many people have long hours to work
You are rich, but you have no friends
So what do you do?
You work like there is no end.

Many people wish for love
But they never get it.
So when you find someone you love
Treat them well
You will never regret it!

—Nick T.

Memories

Lost or found, memories live on
Sometimes forgotten,
Sometimes remembered
Do with them what you wish
For they are yours to possess.

Whether you cherish them or hate them
They are yours as they come with experience
They are not to be taken for granted
Lost or found, memories live on.

—Robert M.

Hold On

Always hold on,
Never let go
Stay true to yourself
Don't doubt what you know

Never let go
Hang on with your might
For if you're confident
It will turn out right.

Stay true to yourself
Try to be strong
Listen to these words
And you'll never go wrong.

Don't doubt what you know
Always stay true
Hold on to your faith
And do what you do.

—Robert M.

Homeless

Sad, dirty, wandering people
Everywhere and nowhere
Smiling, squatting, staring
Lying on benches, pushing shopping carts
Wearing tattered clothes
With empty eyes and restless hands
Where do you go?

If home is where the heart is...
Do the homeless have no heart?

—Franz L.

I Wouldn't

I wouldn't say I'm lonely
I wouldn't say I miss you
But every time I think of you
I need another tissue.

—Rachel D.

Who Said

Who said "Love is Life"
That it's better to have loved and lost
Than never to have loved at all
That there is Life after Love?

Who said that Love is great
That Love is deeper than deep
That loving leaves no doubt.
I DID!!!

—Nick T.

FYI

WHO? EVERYONE
WHAT? FAITH
WHERE? IN CHRIST
WHY? JOHN 3:16
WHEN? NOW AND FOREVER

—Nick T.

Memory

Memory – It's why we can experience the exhilaration of the stage
Memory - It's why we see their faces and hear their voices after they are gone
Memory - It's why we can forgive but cannot forget
Memory – It's why we can hum a cheerful tune without music
Memory – It's why we can have sunshine on a cloudy day
Memory – It's why we can have roses in wintertime

—Cassie P.

The Purpose of a Dream

A dream is to want
A dream is to follow
A dream puts you on a path
That keeps life from being hollow
You may not succeed
But you never know
One day your dream
Might just come true

—Andrew R.

Beautiful Girl

Beautiful is she beyond the trees
Watching her there – hair blowing in the breeze
I saw her yesterday, sitting in the sand
If only I had the courage to hold her hand
Beautiful is she as she passes this way
Hold tight to my heart – she can steal it away.

—Andrew R.

Life

Life is funny
Life is sad
Life will make you happy
But also make you mad

Life is dirty
Life is clean
Life will make you smile
But also make you scream

Life is boring
Life is exciting
Life will make you predictable
But also make you surprising

Life is good
Life is bad
Life will make you frustrated
But be thankful for the life you've had

—Robin M.

Making Poems

Poems are fun to make
If you have the right frame of mind
But you have to think and it might take some time
Write ... Stop
Write ... Stop
Think ...Pop!
Something else. Another good thought!
If you have a strong base
You can write like mad
Whether the mood of the poem
Is glad, funny, or sad.
These are some things
You might want to know
If you want to write poems
Just like a pro.

—Robert M.

Fingernails

Fingernails are varied
It's plain enough to see
Some are neatly manicured
Polished, neat and clean.
Others are wild
Some long, some short
Painted, striped, strangely filed.
Still others are humble
Unadorned but for dirt
Lying in creases caused by a stumble.
These varied fingernails have stories to tell
About people's lives and where people dwell

—Robin M.

The Wallflower

She looks around and doesn't say much
Even though there's a lot on her mind
She wants to talk but has no touch
Talking to guys -
she's just not the kind.

She doesn't say much to anybody
She's far too afraid to speak
Since people think she's a nobody
Her life is bleak.

She has many skills
But she's not comfortable sharing
In her life there are no thrills
Because she doesn't know caring.

Whenever you see her, she is alone
She prefers to cower
And silently groan
She is a wallflower.

—Gus S.

Poetry Schmoetry

This is one thing
I don't know how to write
While I'm thinking
I might as well get a Sprite.

This rhymes with that
That rhymes with this
If poetry was easy
This would be bliss.

Oh, my gosh!
I somehow made a rhyme
Hey, maybe this won't
Take so much time.

HaHaHa! I'm a poet
And I didn't know it
There it goes again
I'm a rhyming fool.

Wow! This poetry stuff
Is actually kind of cool!

—Tanner E.

Listen to your Momma

Momma said not to make faces
Or I'd get stuck that way
I didn't believe her
Now I look like a beaver.

—Steven C.

Popped Quiz

"Okay class, put your books away
We're having a pop quiz today."
The teacher said as she entered the room
Warning the class of impending doom.
"Oh no!' Josh thought, "This has to be stopped!"
And to his relief...
The pop quiz popped!

—Steven C.

Red

The color of rebels
The color of choice
The color of embarrassment
The color with a voice

The color of love
The color of fire
The color of flowers
The color I desire

The color of the 49ers
The color of the flag by my bed
The color of heartache tears
The color of bloodshed

—Gus S.

City of Lights

Different sights and different sounds
People from all over walking around
Many a color, size, and shape
Everyone wants to visit this beautiful place
Total freedom of expression being displayed
Dancing and singing and selling their trades
The wind is blowing the scent of the bay
The sea lions are barking and fresh bread being baked
The ships begin to sound their horns
The fog is rolling in; they better get ashore
Warm clam chowder will soon fill you bellies
Then later you can take a ride on the trolleys
Take a ride and see the sights
Through the city of San Francisco
The City of Lights

—Franz L.

WEAVE YOUR OWN THOUGHTS

WEAVE YOUR OWN THOUGHTS

WEAVE YOUR OWN THOUGHTS

INTRODUCTION TO
PRICELESS GIFTS

Christmas was coming. Gifts, presents, and delicious food … a time to look forward to with excitement.

I gave my students a writing prompt that would capture this time of year but with a twist.

"Write about what you would like to receive for Christmas and what you would like to give others for Christmas; however, <u>these gifts may not cost any money</u> ."

The kids looked bewildered, but as they processed the prompt, I could see ideas popping into their minds, and the pencils started moving. Little did I realize, their responses would share amazing glimpses into their hearts, souls, and minds.

As you read these student voices, my prayer is that you recall where your own thoughts were during that time in your life. I also pray you will open your heart, soul, and mind to the children in your life.

Look deeply. Reflect. Accept.

PRICELESS GIFTS

1. *I would love to give my parents what they deserve. My parents have done everything in the world for me; they don't give me what I want; they give me what I need. And what I'm going to give my parents is lots of love and respect.*

   What I want for Christmas is my family together because I really miss my mom, my baby sister, and my annoying little brother. I love them with all my heart, and I count the days 'til I see them again. I LOVE YOU, MOM!!!

2. *I would like to have peace in my family any time of the year. I want peace because without it, me, my mama, and my brother stress out. Also, if there was peace my mama wouldn't get hurt anymore, and me and my brother wouldn't have to see our mama cry.*

   I would like to give my mama courage and strength to overcome her hardships. I know she would like that because she doesn't have to tell me when she's sad for me to know. If I could give her more courage, I think she would really like it.

3. *The wonderful gift I would like to receive this year for a Merry Christmas is actually not for me, but for others. It does have a cost still though. The cost is a change in the way people treat others. Instead of being rude and inconsiderate to people that they might think are weird or "different", I wish people would be kind and accept them for who they are and maybe even realize that sometimes different is good. If people do that, the nice and heartwarming gift they will get back is a friendship – a new person to party with, do each other's hair, share secrets, and more with.*

4. *I would like to give everyone blind their sight back, but in return I would like all divorces to get back together. I would like this because*

divorce has been a big part of my life with my grandparents and my own parents, which has brought very stressful times.

5. *This year for Christmas I don't want to receive anything special except the happiness my dad will share when he gets the job he's always yearned for. That is the only thing I want for Christmas. It is also part of my Christmas wish for my dad to get at least one thing special in his hardworking life.*

   The gift I would like to give is a storytelling or a song sung by my friend and myself for the unfortunate orphans of Manteca. It would at least brighten their eyes. For the exciting experience of being with people who care about them is one I would not forget.

6. *The gift I would like to receive would be nothing. I'm just fine with what I have right now. I already have a family and friends that I love and I wouldn't change it for a thing. Now I might not have a home yet but at least I have somewhere to sleep every night. I have clothes to wear every day, and that's all I need! I'm so grateful for everything and everyone I have, and I don't need anything else.*

   The gift I would give someone else would be for those who don't have a family, home, or clothes. But since I can't use money on the gift, I pray for them who don't have much.

7. *I don't really need a gift because I have everything a child could hope for: loving parents, a bed to sleep in, warmth for my body, and food in my stomach. Some kids out there would pray to have those four simple things. This technology now has corrupted our minds into thinking we need all those expensive things when in fact we don't.*

   The gift I would love to give is things to the homeless. My family and I want to go out this year for Christmas and provide them with clothes and blankets so that they don't freeze in these cold winter nights.

8. *I would like to receive a present; I've been waiting for years; the chance to see my dad. I miss him so much. I liked it when I would see him; he would pick me up and just squeeze me until my back cracked. That's how much he missed me. That is why I would like to have this present. The gift I would give is just to be a good son to my parents and let them know that I love them and try to be the greatest big brother that I can be. That is what I would give to my brothers and parents.*

9. *This year I would like to receive peace. No more family problems. I just wish we could all be happy. With just that gift I would be happy this Christmas. I'm sad knowing that I won't talk to my mom this Christmas, but I have to keep away. I would also like to see my grandma one more time; just see her smile once again. It's the third Christmas without her here. That would make my Christmas so special!*

10. *I would give a gift of a smile every day to my parents to show them I'm OK. Also even if I'm growing I will always be their monkey, forever, no matter what happens to me. To show my parents not to worry about me, just to worry about themselves.*

11. *A gift I would give someone is respect. It doesn't take much. I wouldn't make fun of them, and I would listen to what they say. I'm pretty sure anybody would be happy with a little respect.*

12. *The gift I would like to receive is the gift of luck from God. May everything I attempt this season of joy, be blessed by Him, and may I succeed in that task.*

The gift I would like to give is the gift of JOY to my family. May I please not do anything that makes me a burden or impels others to do what they might later regret. Let me "create" smiles and give them to my family.

13. *A gift I would like to give would be happiness to all because not everyone has happiness in life. And I think that everyone should be happy all the time.*
    A gift I would like to receive is love because I'm not all that loved all the time. Plus, I love to be loved a lot. I know it sounds crazy but it's true.

14. *The gift I would like to receive is nothing more but to be with my family. I just want to celebrate this wonderful time of the year knowing that I can be grateful to God for giving me such a wonderful family.*

15. *The gift I'd like to receive would be to get to know my dad's family better.*
    The gift I'd like to give would be better health for my mom's friend who has cancer.

16. *As you all know, Christmas is not about the material things that you give or receive, It's about love, family, and everyone coming together to spend a precious day with one another. So would you like to know what I want for Christmas this year? My family is not very close. Sometimes I even go months, even years without seeing them. As kids we were all so close. But as the years went by and we got older we've kind of drifted away from each other. So, this year for Christmas I want to be closer with my family. I hope that's not asking too much.*
    And as for giving, I would like to give my dad, well, good health if I

could, but just being there for him, and helping him with whatever he needs. It may not be much, but that's what I think he'll love the best.

17. *A gift that I would like to receive is the gift of patience because sometimes when my brother really gets me mad I always seem to say something unkind back to him. And I would really just like to have the patience not to say anything at all and just let it go.*

18. *A gift that I would like to receive for Christmas is more appreciation from people because I try hard and do my best but I don't receive the appreciation I deserve. So that is what I would like for Christmas. And in return I will give more happiness and also appreciation toward others.*

19. *A gift I would like to receive would be love. I would like love because I want to know that someone cares. Another reason I chose love is because I could talk to someone who would listen and not ignore me. This is why I chose love as my gift to receive for Christmas.*

20. *A gift I would like to receive is my family's wellbeing to get only better. We are going through a tough time, and it's really hard on my parents. It would be wonderful to know their minds are at ease.*
    A gift I would like to give is a song. I've been working on my piano, and I would like to finish the song for my mom and dad: all that's left is putting the lyrics in order. I hope it will be the kind of song that will make you cry in a good way.

21. *For Christmas I want to go live with my mom in Oregon, but my dad won't let me. For Christmas I would like to give my dad the best son he could ask for. I won't talk back. If he tells me to do something, I'll do it the first time he asks.*

22. The gift I would like to receive from my mom is love…

23. For Christmas, I'd like to receive the gift of patience, so I can learn to deal with my younger siblings better; so I can take time to listen to them and not always get upset when they cry.
For Christmas I would like to give to my mom the gift of understanding… so she will be able to listen and understand what I am trying to talk to her about…hoping that every once in a while, we can have a decent conversation where she doesn't get mad or upset with me.

24. This year for Christmas out of all the gifts I'm getting, the one I would like to have most of all is joy. Being able to just enjoy this holiday and seeing smiles on my family's faces. Just watching my little brothers tear through their presents would put a smile on my face.

25. A gift I would like to receive for Christmas this year would be a hug or even a hello from my family in Mexico. I haven't seen them in a year already so it would be nice to see them.
A gift I would like to give is an invite to a Christmas party to all those people who don't have shelter, food, or nice clothes. It would be nice for them to feel the Christmas joy. They wouldn't feel lonely either. So that's what I would like to receive and give for Christmas.

26. The gift I would like to give is happiness. I would like to give happiness to all the orphan children…the ones who don't have a family to celebrate Christmas with. They don't get to share smiles and love with their moms and dads. I'd really like them to be happy for Christmas. Just think about your loved ones and how happy you are on Christmas day. It would be amazing to know that you shared that happiness with others, too.

27. I want to give my mom love and comfort because of all she is going
through.
Also the gift I would like to get is relief from what impact my family
has taken.

28. I would like the gift of seeing my dad for the first time in six years.
I would like to give the gift of a mechanical leg to my grandpa. He has
lost his leg due to diabetes.

29. The gift I would like to receive is my mom. If I could just see if she is OK
and all right ... maybe be back in my life and make up for the three
years she missed out on.
The gift I would like to give is my love to my mom and show her that
I care about her still. I love her the way she is and that I miss her to
death. Nothing will ever change that. No one can replace you, Mom. I
love you!

30. What I would like to receive for Christmas is for my IQ to go to the
highest it could go. I have been struggling in math. Things are mounting
a lot faster than what I can handle.
I want to give thanks to all my teachers that I've had. Thank-you for
sharing your knowledge with me and your patience. All I could say is
thank-you and have a Merry Christmas.

31. It's the season for giving and some receiving. I'll be honest, I like getting
presents a lot more that I do giving them. That doesn't mean that I never
give presents though.
A gift I would like to receive this year is time with my brother. I have
not seen him in over a year. I talk to him on the phone sometimes, but

I still miss him. He is my best friend and will always be my best friend. We go through tough times like most brothers do, but he's always there for me. I love my big brother.

The point of this paper is getting away from our selfish ways. It's not always about material gain or only getting things. Maybe if we all spread a little joy and love, the world wouldn't be in so much chaos.

32. *What I would give to my family is honesty, respect, and the amount of love that they deserve because they have been nothing but good to me. I have told lies and been bad many times. Now it's time to change. I want to start a new beginning with my family.*

   What do I want? I already got it ... my loving and caring family. They are good people. We may not be the best family in the world, but I'll tell you something, we do love; we do care. All I want from them is a new beginning, another chance to show them that I do care for them. I've changed tremendously, Mom, sisters, Grandma, and Grandpa. I love you all with all my heart ... Merry Christmas!

33. *What I would like to receive for Christmas is for my family and friends to get along more and not fight.*

   What I would like to give for Christmas is the true meaning of Christmas because all everyone wants is presents, but Christmas is about when Jesus was born and about family and friends having fun and peace.

34. *I would like to give more than just things such as toys and materialistic things. But instead I would rather give love and caring to the ones I trust the most.*

   I would give these things to my family like my mom for at least trying to raise me and to my dad for the few good times I had. I would especially like to give the best Christmas to my Grandma because she took me in and didn't let me go to foster care ... and give tons of thanks to God.

35. *What I would like to receive for Christmas is for my dad not to get drunk for one night and not yell at us ... for him to be supportive and hug me ... to have it snow ... to make a snowman.*
I would like to give my mom and dad good grades like A's and B's. I would like to give my sister something awesome like love and hugs.

36. *This year I would like to receive nothing about me ... I'd just like my Grandpa to be healed from his cancer and be able to do things like he used to.*
This year, I'd like to give courage to everybody trying to stop something ... like when people say they can't do it, let them know they can, just let them know there is someone who believes in them. Because I hear people say "I can't" or they just give up a lot lately.

37. *What I'd like to receive is my Grandpa's appearance one last time before he passed away a few months ago. I rarely got to see him because he lived so far away. And when I did get to see him he was always sick. So I would like to see my grandpa one last time. I'd also like to help my grandma; she has cancer right now.*

38. *I would like to receive more recognition for my work from my parents. I hardly get awarded for my work, but then again they're too busy. But as long as they thank me, it's okay because I know they love me. That's something I want for Christmas.*
What I want to give for Christmas is more social time with my parents. I have to say, I hardly spend time with my parents at all except when

we travel to places or when it's just them and me. I really want to spend more time since Dad always comes home late from work. This is what I'd like for Christmas and a couple of presents.

39. *Merry Christmas. This holiday season I would like to give my family the gift of love and happiness. Sometimes I don't always show them how much I love and appreciate them. So I would like to change that and show my family how much they mean to me. At times I'm not happy, and I take my anger out on them. That's wrong to do though so I would like to try my best at not doing that.*
If I could receive one special gift this year it would be to stop fighting with my mom. I want this gift because when me and my mom fight then we aren't happy. I need to try my best to listen to her instead of arguing. That would be one amazing gift that I will try to achieve.

40. *What I would like to receive is some more time with my family. Mostly my dad because he works a lot and it's hard on him. So not so much a gift for me but for him. I also wish for Christmas that my family was still happily together. I also wish for my mom to do the right thing.*
What I would like to give my dad for Christmas is a good, obedient daughter who does the dishes without being asked and keeping the house clean so when he gets home from a long hard day of work he can relax. Also I would like to give my mom a better conscience.

41. *What I would like to receive for Christmas is for my dad to get better. He has been ill for over a year. Everyday he takes medicine to keep him alert. Doctors have done surgery on his head, but it left him paralyzed in his left arm and leg. He has gotten better every month, but I just want him to go back to the way he was.*

I would like to give somebody a ... Christmas ... someone who doesn't have all that I have.

42. *What I would like to receive for Christmas is loyalty and trust and that is all I really ask for because not every little thing is about money.*
And what I ask for in return is a little bit of trustworthiness and some love.

43. *What I would like to receive for Christmas is for my dad to be home at Christmas.*
What I would like to receive for Christmas is a family that would love me even when I'm bad.

44. *What I would like to receive is my dad to come home for Christmas because he hasn't been home in about three months, and this will be our first Christmas without him.*
I would like to give everyone in my house a very wonderful Christmas because my dad can't be here. My little sister is going to be so sad.

45. *I would like to receive love and caring so I don't feel left out like I usually do.*
In return I would give full respect to my dad ... and help around the house. I would do whatever he says without fighting.

46. *Something I would like to get for Christmas would be to spend time with my brother and my dad because I never get to see them ever since my brother moved to go to college, and my dad left when I was seven. Usually when my whole family was together we had a good time, like "old times".*

I would give my mom a present by cleaning my room because supposedly it's messy but I like the way it is.

47. *I would give thanks to Jesus for my life and everything that I have. I would also give thanks to God. I would ask for nothing in return.*

48. *Imagine if Christmas never existed. Most kids would think, "Then you wouldn't get any presents". How about getting or giving a present that doesn't cost money? ... something that is given by attitude.*
    If I could choose something to give, it would probably be to treat my brother as a brother. My parents are always telling me, "Be nice to your brother" or, "You need to start treating him better". Lately I haven't been treating him poorly, but I think I can stop yelling and pinching him.
    What I would like to receive is very easy to guess. For Christmas I would like for my father to get his health back. For the past four months he's had pneumonia and leukemia. I rarely see him because I'm at school, and he's always on our couch sleeping. The only time I talk to him is if I'm helping him or he wants me to feed the dog. So for Christmas, I would like my dad to get well.

49. *The gift I would like to receive is a card or a phone call from my godparents who never call on my birthday or Christmas, and I never see. The gift I'm going to give is to my parents. They are going to wake up to the sound of me vacuuming and cleaning the house.*

50. *For many people it's hard to think about presents that don't cost money. For me, it's easy. The one gift to give from me to friends and family is the gift of love. Love is not selfish; love is not jealous; love is not hatred. Love is kind; love is caring for someone that loves you. That is one thing*

that friends and family can share year-round. Love helps heal the soul. It can soothe the burn of hate.

51. *The one thing I would like to receive is the gift of support. I don't really have much support from my family. Mom and grandma don't like my career choices ... Some support would help a lot. It would make me feel like I'm not just another face in the crowd.*

52. *If I could receive something for Christmas it would be a life just for me ... life with no worries ... no violence ... no competition ... no troubled times.*
   If I could give a gift to anyone it would be to my family. I would give them all the love in the world because they mean the most to me and the world to me.

53. *One gift I would like to get for Christmas is knowing that my brother actually cares about me. I would choose this because during high school he would ignore me, lock me out of his room, and he would always cheat me out of things.*

54. *The gift I want is my dad. I haven't seen him in a long time. He is in jail. He gets out this month. That is going to be my favorite present for Christmas.*
   I want to give him good grades and a better attitude for Christmas. He will be so happy when I do change my grades and attitude.

55. *The gift I would like to receive would be to take away my diabetes because I don't really like seeing blood three times a day. I really hope my diabetes goes away soon.*

The gift I would give would be more love and compassion to everyone even though I've been nice in a way. But I want to be nicer because I want people to know I'm nice.

56. *If I could give anything to anybody … I would pick my brother, because he has really bad asthma. I would take that away from him. Whenever he wants to go outside, me or my mom have to give him a breathing treatment. So it's a long process for him to do something.*
   One gift I would like to receive is for my dad to move back from Texas. He lives there with his new wife and kids now, and I haven't seen him in 2 years so it's been a long time. He has one girl and one boy, and he forgot about me and my brother.

57. *Christmas is coming and we always have to tell our parents what we want. This Christmas I asked for a lot of things, but what I really want does not cost any money. I want to see my dad again because I have not seen him in two years. It would mean the world to me if I saw my dad again.*
   I also want to give a very special gift to my mom and that would be love. My mom works so very hard to care for us, and I think she needs to be loved and appreciated more.

58. *The gift I would like to receive from the Lord Himself is to have a great conversation with Him. The reason for that gift is because I want to see Him in person and to just talk to Him, but people say you talk to Him when you pray. Another reason is because the Lord Himself is almighty and just imagine talking to Him. That would be the greatest gift ever, I think.*
   The gift I would like to give would be freedom to all the slaves around the world. The reason for that is because I think it is unfair for some

people to have freedom while others are tortured. Why do some people have to be tortured while others don't? Freedom ... that is the gift I would like to give.

59. *The gift I would like to receive is the gift of hope. I just want my parents to love me for who I am. I know they have given up on me a lot of my life, and I give up on them sometimes. I know I can do a lot more; I just don't know how to start. Everything I do is not good enough compared to my sister. I know they love me; I just hope they know I love them ... all I need is hope!*

60. *For Christmas, I would like to give thanks to my parents for what they have done. They both work hard to give us things we don't need but we want. My parents need to know that I like them for who they are, not the things we get from them. I am going to tell them that I love them for the good things in life that is worth living for.*
    For Christmas I would like to get lots of love. Because my parents are focused on trips, jobs, bills to pay, they don't have time to give attention to kids. They do care, but they don't spend time with me. I just want more time with them. I'm not saying I want just to have love but joy also.
    The gift I would like to receive would just be less fighting. All I sorta want is peace. I don't know why I want it, possibly just so I won't hear a lot of complaining and screaming.

61. *The gift I would like to get is peace. Often times my sister bothers me and goes digging through my stuff.*
    A gift that I would give is honesty. For numerous times or a couple times I have lied to my parents. It is important that a parent can trust their own kids. A little honesty may be a good way to start.

62. *I would really like to give my best behavior because I know it would mean a lot to my mom. I will get along with my brothers, and I would also make sure she is having a good time because lately she has been worrying about money.*

63. *One gift that I would like to receive, that costs no actual money or price is to see my mother happy, seeing her father one last time, for a second, a minute, an hour or a day. For her to see him alive just one more time. I would like to receive this because I love my mom.*

    After my grandpa passed away this year, it opened my eyes to what life is really about. I realized that life doesn't go on forever, so you can't take anybody or anything for granted. I have to think … I don't even talk to my dad. My mom is all I have, literally. She does the best she can and that's enough. You have to tell your loved ones, including your friends, how much they mean to you before it's too late. Yeah … maybe it seems more about my mom than for me, but it's what I want.

    One gift I would like to give that I wish I could give is for the Africans and everyone else who's slowly but painfully dying of starvation to have food, clothes, and shelter. I would like to do this because before me and my mother didn't have a home to call "our own", but she kept on praying and within a week we got an apartment. Other people have it much worse than us. I know for a fact at times we all take things for granted. That's why I give thanks and pray before I eat.

64. *For Christmas, I don't expect much though I would really like my family to make me a card. I would like a card because it costs no money or greed, and you can cherish it forever.*

    I would like to give friendship this Christmas. I'd like to make someone feel loved and cared for. Friendship is a great gift if you know how to give it.

65. *The gift I would like to give is a day that's normal with my brothers. We sometimes fight about who gets to play first.*

    The gift I would like to receive is to see my uncle from Mexico. He got deported last year. When I found out he was deported I kinda just felt like I was in a rough spot. I just want to see him again.

WEAVE YOUR OWN THOUGHTS

WEAVE YOUR OWN THOUGHTS

WEAVE YOUR OWN THOUGHTS

CLASSROOM
STORIES

CLASSROOM STORIES

*T*he third strand in our tapestry moves from student voices to stories from the classroom. We will look at how instruction from a time of little technology to a time of rampant technology affected the classroom, lessons that challenged the students' minds, and personal stories of students who were dealing with tragic situations.

1. **AIN'T TECHNOLOGY GREAT?**
   Serious consequences of phones in the classroom.

2. **DISTRIBUTE THE WEALTH**
   What sounds good and how it works are often two very different things.

3. **YOU CAN'T DO THAT, MS. DEJONG! YOU'LL GET IN TROUBLE**
   What happened when I told the students to bring their Bibles to school.

4. **NOT SO DIFFERENT AFTER ALL**
   Parent-teacher conferences can be interesting!

5. **THEN HOW DO YOU KNOW HE LOVES YOU?**
   Be cautious about what you show kids and then call love.

6. **WHAT KIND OF SMART ARE YOU?**

Be careful not to put others down because they are smart in a different way than you are.

7. **GRACE**
The age-old question … Why does God let bad things happen?

8. **JIMMY'S RESILIENCE**
Despite everything, Jimmy kept living his life well.

9. **… AND GIVE TONS OF THANKS TO GOD!**
Making lemonade out of lemons.

~1~

AIN'T TECHNOLOGY GREAT?

I decided I needed a break from writing, so I clicked over to my Facebook page. The first entry I saw was an interview with a psychologist who was talking about the impact of technology on kids in the age bracket that I was teaching—twelve-to-fourteen year olds. She said that she had seen a 50 percent increase in depression and a substantial increase in the suicide rate. The specific years mentioned were 2011–2012. These were the years when the number of kids who had iPhones exceeded the 50 percent mark. I taught through those years. Her observations accurately reflected what I saw in my classroom.

This was in the early 2000s. Kids were just beginning to get their own cell phones, and of course, bringing them to school, and of course, using them at school, which was, of course, against the rules. I must tell you—cell phones were the bane of my existence as a junior high teacher. The following story is one of the reasons why.

Emma, a young girl in my class, was very needy. She had already had some drug issues and was failing all her classes. She did not have a father in her life but did have a mother who found refuge in many men, a far too common recipe for disaster.

Emma had potential; she loved to write but was too undisciplined to finish and turn in assignments. Her only reason for attending school was wrapped up in her boyfriend, John, who was her only solace. School was their meeting place.

Sue, a classmate, also liked Emma's boyfriend. One day, Sue decided to go into the bathroom with her iPhone at recess, take off her top and bra, and take some "selfies." (I don't think that term had even been coined at that time.) During the next class period, she sent these pictures to John, who promptly decided to dump Emma and ask Sue to be his girlfriend.

OK, typical junior high drama. I get it, but there is more to the story.

At lunchtime, John told Emma that he was breaking up with her. He wanted Sue to be his girlfriend. Emma, in her fragile emotional state, was unable to handle this.

Meanwhile, I was in the teacher's lounge eating lunch when the bells went off. I rushed outside to find Emma laying on a bench with yard duty aides around her, calling for help. Emma had taken a knife and cut her wrists. The police and an ambulance came and took her to the hospital. She was physically OK but in deep emotional pain.

Emma returned to school a few days later, still troubled, and very embarrassed. She was sent to counseling and put in a special class for emotionally disturbed students.

This did not solve her problems.

~2~

DISTRIBUTE THE WEALTH

*O*ne thing I learned about junior high kids is that they are keenly tuned in to what is fair. While they don't always act fair themselves, they are very critical of anyone else not acting fairly. Come to think about it, that's not exclusive to junior high kids.

A few years back, the idea of distribution of wealth became a popular political football. Some kids thought it was fair. Others thought everyone should keep what they had worked for.

I decided the best way for the kids to understand the principle was to apply it to the classroom. The "wealth" to be distributed was their grades. If your grade was 90 and another student's grade was 50, then you would owe twenty points to the student with 50. Both would then receive a grade of 70 for the assignment.

The next assignment I returned to the students had two grades. The first grade was their personally earned grade; the other was their "distributed" grade. For example, 98/67 meant that the student who did the assignment earned a score of 98, but after distributing points to make the scores even, they would get a final grade of 67. On the contrary, a score of 43/67 meant that the student doing the assignment earned a score of 43, but after distributing points to make them even, they would receive a score of 67 since every student would receive the class average grade.

Positive and negative reactions lined up just as I expected they would. The high scoring students were upset. The low scoring students, especially the ones who did not do the assignment, were quite happy.

When a spelling/vocabulary assignment was given the next day, the first question a student asked was how the assignment would be graded. I said that we would be "distributing the wealth."

It was usual for four to six kids out of thirty-two not to do the assignment. This time, twelve did not turn in the assignment, and the average grade dropped to around 50. I returned the assignment and told them how much the grades had dropped.

I asked the kids to write in their learning logs what they thought of "distribution of wealth" after our experiment.

The responses went something like this:

"I didn't try too hard 'cuz I knew I would get someone's points."

"I didn't do it. I don't want someone else getting my points that I earned."

One student summed it up pretty well: "I sometimes don't do my work so getting points from students that get good grades seemed like a cool idea. But it really isn't fair. So I don't feel too good about my grade."

I was pleasantly surprised by that statement: "So I really don't feel too good about my grade." Rather than being pleased about getting points he did not earn, he lost a sense of accomplishment.

A few days later, I gave the kids an opportunity to earn extra credit by doing a project on a novel we were studying. Jimmy, a top student, asked, "If I do the extra credit work, will you take some of my points and give them to another student?"

"What if I said 'no,' you will keep all your points?" I asked.

"Then I'll do it," he said.

"What if I said 'yes,' some of your points will be given to other students?"

"Then I'm not going to do it!" he said firmly with his arms crossed across his chest.

That little exchange summarized the results of "the distribution of wealth" experiment in my class.

First, the overall quality and quantity of work dropped dramatically and quickly.

Second, the brightest refused to go above and beyond, thereby not allowing others to benefit from their abilities.

Thirdly, those who received points they did not earn were not proud and lost a sense of accomplishment.

Lesson learned! Everybody loses!

~3~

BRING YOUR BIBLES
TO SCHOOL

"Y ou can't do that, Ms. DeJong. You'll get in trouble!"

Not exactly what you would expect a junior high student to say to a teacher. A teacher might say that to a student, but a student worried about her teacher getting in trouble?

Why did they think that I would get in trouble?

Well, I told the kids we were going to study Genesis 3 in the Bible and that they could bring their Bibles to school and read directly from the source.

That's when I heard, "You can't do that, Ms. DeJong. You'll get in trouble!"

Being a Christian in the United States is interesting. Being a Christian in the public schools in the United States is really interesting! By the way, there are many of us in public schools.

For most of my thirty-three-year teaching career, although I was a Christian, I followed the "party line" of not saying anything about "that" part of my life. Indeed, I dropped my Christian beliefs at the schoolhouse door and walked into my classroom sans my Christianity.

That's not to say I didn't follow my Christian beliefs in actions, but I did not talk about them. No! No! No! Like Mary's little lamb coming to school, that would be against the rules!

Now, I never "saw" those rules in black and white. It was all conveyed in shades of gray: you can't mention "God," you can't talk about the Bible, and you certainly can't allow students to read the Bible at school. But because everyone seemed so concerned about it, I erred on the side of caution and followed the unwritten rules.

How did I get to the point of asking my kids to bring their Bibles to school?

In 2008, I attended a workshop, "Faith, Freedom, and Public Schools," led by Eric and Kim Buehrer. Their mission is to shed the light of *truth* about what can and cannot be done legally in a public classroom when it comes to matters of faith.

Attending that workshop revolutionized my teaching! I learned a lot. But the most important thing I learned was a plumb line for what I could legally do and say in my classroom *and* what I could not legally do and say.

It lies in the fact that there is a difference between teaching "about" and teaching "in."

Teaching "about" is instructional. It studies a thing or concept in its context, gives information about it, and discusses its influence, completely following the guidelines given by the US Department of Education.

Teaching "in" is devotional. It seeks belief and commitment from the student to the thing or concept being studied.

No longer did I have to leave my beliefs in the parking lot each morning. I could walk into my classroom as a whole person and still be within all the legal and academic boundaries.

Now that's true American freedom! That's what this country was settled on. That's what we fought wars over. That's why people still escape from other countries and risk so much to enter ours.

Many emotions flowed through me. I was angry that I had slipped on the slippery gray slope of veiled lies told by the political and educational establishments. I was even angrier that our whole country had slipped down that slope. I was ecstatic that there was a legal truth that proved the slippery slope was a lie. I was frustrated because I wanted the whole world to know the truth. And I was thankful to God that He had put me in a classroom where I could teach within this truth.

With this newfound truth, I did some researching. I found that a language arts classroom allows more opportunity to discuss "controversial" ideas than a science or math class, which basically deals with facts. Also, if there was an allusion in a story, a teacher could teach about the origin of that allusion.

An opportunity to apply this new knowledge came about as we were reading a short story, "Flowers for Algernon," in our state-adopted ELA textbook.

Briefly, it's the story about Charley, a mentally delayed man, who has a chance to undergo a brain surgery that will increase his intelligence to the genius level. He does so, but as he gains intelligence, he loses friends. A lady working in the factory where Charley sweeps floors tells Charley he should have been happy with the way he was before the surgery.

She tells Charley that he should have been satisfied with the way he was, using Eve in the garden of Eden as an illustration. Eve was tempted by Satan, who promised her that she could have more than she already had, and as a result, we all suffer from sin because of her disobedience to God.

I asked my students if they knew what the lady in the story was referring to. Almost all of them raised their hands. "It's about Adam and Eve in the garden of Eden."

"How do you know that?" I asked.

Answers varied. "I learned it at church, Sunday school, confirmation classes, etc."

I asked what they knew about the story. Many raised their hand. "It's about the devil tempting Adam and Eve in the garden and causing them to sin."

"How many of you have actually read it in the Bible?" Fewer students raised their hands, explaining that they had only heard the story. "Would you like to read the story directly from the Bible?"

They looked a little confused and mumbled, "Yeah, OK, maybe …"

I told them to bring their Bibles to school and that we would read the story together in class.

That's when I got the warning: "You can't do that, Ms. DeJong. You'll get in trouble!"

Out of respect for my principal, I told him my plans and explained their legality and academic purpose. If he were to get any questions, he would already know about the lesson and how to respond. He thanked me for telling him and told me to enjoy the lesson.

The next morning before school began, I was sitting at my desk when I heard a knock on the door. I opened the door to find a student standing there with her backpack open. She took out her Bible, keeping it under cover, and whispered, "Look, I brought my Bible. Are you sure it's OK?" I assured her it was. She walked over to her desk, setting her Bible right on top.

The bell rang, and the rest of the students came in and sat down. After the morning routine, we began our lesson. Students who had brought their Bibles opened them to Genesis 3, and I passed out copies of the passage to the others.

The interest and curiosity were evident from the questions the students asked. I threw each question back to the students for their input: If Eve ate the "apple," why does Adam get the blame?

- What if Eve said "no" to the serpent?
- What if Eve ate the "apple" but Adam said "no"?
- Why did God even allow Satan into the Garden?
- Why does everyone say Eve was tricked by the serpent? It says in Genesis 3:2 that she knew exactly what the rules were.
- Why did God even make rules for Adam and Eve in the Garden?
- Why do we all have to suffer for a bad choice that they made?

We identified four basic strategies that Satan used:

1. First, he caused Eve to **doubt** God's words, i.e. "Did God really say …" (v. 1).
2. Next, he openly **denies** God's words, i.e. "You will not surely die …" (v. 4).
3. Finally, he **distorts** God's words by appealing to her pride, i.e. "For God knows that when you eat of it your eyes will be opened, and you will be like God, knowing good and evil" (v. 5).
4. This results in a **desire** within Eve to experience what God's words have clearly set beyond her boundary of obedience to God's authority.

A journal assignment followed: Identify situations in which you have been tempted with the same strategies that Satan used with Eve.

The students had no trouble thinking of situations to write about. They easily identified strategies they had heard or used themselves:

1. **Doubt**—"Did your parents really say …?" "I don't think the teacher expects that."
2. **Denial**—"You won't get in trouble." "Nobody will know."
3. **Distortion**—"Just one beer won't hurt you." "One time will be OK."
4. **Desire**—"I know I shouldn't cheat, but I didn't study, and my friend said I could copy his paper."

We did this lesson together in class—a public school classroom. It completely followed the academic and religious freedom guidelines given by the US Department of Education.

We all enjoyed the lesson, and we were all relived that I did not get in trouble.

~4~

NOT SO DIFFERENT AFTER ALL

Alone

I am alone in this nightmare
No one to hold me, no one to care
No one to talk to, no one to share
Please hold me someone
Please someone care.

I'm sure we can all relate to the loneliness described in this poem that was written by a boy in my class.

Rereading this poem reminded me of a mother who came in to talk to me—actually, yell at me—about the failing grades I was "giving" her son, and who claimed that it was my fault he would not graduate. (My class was not the only one he was failing.) The first trimester report cards had been passed out, and his report card indicated he would not be able to graduate due to his grades.

The school secretary called me to warn me the mother was on her way to my classroom. I nervously waited for her to arrive. Her pounding on the door let me know she was there.

From the way she walked in the room and her refusal to sit when I offered her a chair, I knew our meeting would not be pleasant.

"Please, sit down," I said as I gestured to a chair across from my desk.

"I'm not here for a friendly visit. I'm here to find out why you're picking on my son."

"OK. Let's look at his grades and last report card to see what's going on." I told her the record book showed he had not turned in eleven out of twenty assignments, and the ones he did turn in were incomplete.

That's when she let me have it. "Do you think all I have to do is monitor the assignments that *you* give him? I have two other children to worry about. I work two jobs and don't have the luxury that you have with your nice clothes and respectable job and regular hours. It's all I can do to buy food and clothes for them … I can't even always do that. You think you are so much better than me because I'm not the perfect parent that you are!"

The tirade continued along these same lines for a little longer. Realizing that she needed to vent, I kept quiet.

After venting for a while, she said she needed a cigarette. As she fumbled in her purse looking for one, I told her I was sorry, but she could not smoke on the school grounds. That started another tirade about how everybody at school was so special that they couldn't be around cigarettes.

Well, that was certainly not the hill I was willing to die on … I remained quiet.

Then she looked up from fumbling in her purse. I could see her eyes welling up with tears. She slumped in the chair and sobbed, "I can't do it anymore. I can't do it anymore. I can't do …"

Everything changed at that moment. All agendas and preconceived judgments, both hers and mine, were gone. Without thinking, I went around my desk and sat next to her. I took her hands in mine, leaned over, and held her. She did not resist.

And then I told her my story. Yes, I was sitting in a classroom as the teacher. But it had not always been so. I shared that I walked the same path that she walked; I was a divorced, single parent. I knew the hopelessness, the depression, the difficulties. And even though it looked to her like I had it all together, I did not!

Silence … She looked at me and mumbled, "Thank you."

We came up with a plan for her son to follow that would allow him to pass my class and get the units he needed for graduation. I met with the two other teachers whose classes he was failing, and they also agreed to make a plan for him. I'll admit I broke some of my ironclad rules about not accepting missing or late assignments. I did not, however, lower the bar on grading his work. He and his mom needed to feel the authentic reward of hard work. To lower my standards for his assignments would be an insult to him and his mother.

Well, he managed to fulfill the requirements that we laid out for him. He was far from graduating at the top of his class, but he did graduate. His mother stepped up a bit by signing his assignments … sometimes.

The next time I saw her was at his graduation. We looked at each other for a moment. She walked up to me and quietly said, "Thank you," and moved on.

It doesn't get better than that!

~5~

THEN HOW DO YOU KNOW HE LOVES YOU?

ood question! A question we should take time to talk about with our kids—boys and girls.

Several years back, a friend of mine told me about a student of hers. She was concerned about this girl in her class, Julie (not her real name), because she had some marks on her that were possibly from abuse. She was also in a very codependent relationship with a male student who was physically aggressive.

My friend asked Julie to come by after school. As they were talking, Julie asked my friend if she was married.

"Yes, I am," my friend responded.

"Does your husband love you?"

"Yes, we love each other," answered my friend.

The next question shocked my friend. "Does he hit you?"

"Of course not."

"Then how do you know he loves you?" Julie asked.

Wow! This girl had associated abuse with love. Please think about how that happens. For most of us, that's shocking. For some, however, that's how they know they are "loved."

How sad!

There are so many roads I could go on from here. I'm not taking any of them. Let this little story take you on your own road. How do you know what love is? What was love when you were thirteen, eighteen, twenty-five, forty …?

Let's take some time to carefully reflect how we are defining love for our children, grandchildren, and others in our sphere of influence.

~6~

WHAT KIND OF "SMART" ARE YOU?

*I*n the 1980s, Howard Gardner, an American developmental psychologist at the Harvard Graduate School of Education, developed a perspective of intelligence called Multiple Intelligences (MI). Briefly, he identified seven (an eighth was added later) areas of intelligence that people possess to one extent or another. As I studied and learned more about this theory, I realized that it expressed and explained what I had noticed about my students' various abilities and preferences in learning and behavior. I found it so interesting and validating to me, not only as a teacher but as a person, that I decided to teach the perspective to my students.

First, we learned about the various intelligences that Gardner had identified:

- Linguistic (word smart)
- Logical-mathematical (number/reasoning smart)
- Musical intelligence (sound smart)
- Visual-spatial (picture smart)

- Bodily-kinesthetic (body smart)
- Interpersonal (people smart)
- Intrapersonal (self-aware smart)
- Nature (surroundings smart)

While explaining the theory to my students and discussing the various "smarts," I would hear, "Wow! that's me," "That's just like Johnny," or "That's my mother." The kids were really interested in the various categories they fit themselves into.

I found several assessments that we could do in class. Watching the students as they discovered what most intuitively knew about themselves was great!

Not only was it validating for the students, it was beneficial for me. As a language arts teacher, I was high in linguistic (word smart). That was the nature of my classroom. But I had many kids whose intelligence preferences were different from mine. Recognizing this removed my tendency to put the various areas of intelligence in a hierarchy with linguistics at the top, and I instead placed them on an equal platform. It changed my tendency to be judgmental and frustrated with students who had difficulty in the intelligence that I was good in. (I'm not proud of that; I just want to be honest that I'm thankful this new perspective corrected my bias.)

Let me share a story that illustrates what I mean. I had a student who was not doing very well in my class. He was trying, but reading and writing were difficult for him. He had scored very high in bodily-kinesthetic (body smart) on the MI assessment. It struck me that while he had difficulty diagramming sentences, I had also watched him on the basketball court right outside my window making long-distance shots and layups that I would never be able to do in a million years. My respect for that young man took on a new perspective. I found that I was much more patient with his classroom difficulties. Feeling accepted for who he was, he was much less anxious about his schoolwork, and his work improved.

This awareness also helped me with coming up with assignments and projects for my students. I found various assignments and projects that complemented the different intelligences and allowed students to choose an assignment that complemented their particular intelligence. If it was a project, they could choose one I had presented or they could present their own suggestion to me. We would then discuss and agree on the project's parameters.

Every year, I taught the novel *Animal Farm* by George Orwell. Two students came to me with a proposal for their final project. They wanted to build the barn and lay out the fields on the farm. They would present it to the class, explaining the different story events that took place in the farm's different areas, and the symbolism of the events. Wow! There was no way they could have understood the story more thoroughly. Doing worksheets, answering comprehension questions, or taking an exam wouldn't have come close!

Other students were inspired to do unique projects. Of course, not all kids did, but they all saw what other students were doing, resulting in secondhand learning. It was a wonderful learning experience, especially for me!

Good things followed that I had not anticipated. Students accepted and validated themselves and each other. They saw their differences as positive, which is not a natural inclination for any of us, particularly in junior high. When we did group projects, they would now seek out partners who had different abilities than themselves, not just their best friends.

I became a more accepting teacher. Rather than being frustrated by students who were not linguistic like me, I admired their diverse abilities, especially those who were gifted in areas that I was not.

Win! Win! Win!

~7~

GRACE

She was a bright student; a little timid and shy but helpful to others, never missed an assignment, and seldom earned less than 100 percent on her schoolwork. Over time, I noticed a change. She became inattentive, although not disruptive. Her assignments were incomplete or not turned in at all. This was not Grace. I wanted to get to the source of the problem, and I knew discipline was not the answer.

One day, I asked her if she would like to eat her lunch with me in my room. Hesitantly, she agreed. We met together. I shared my concerns about her and asked if there was anything I could do.

Her response surprised me.

She asked if I was a Christian. I told her I was. Then she asked that famous question: "Why does God let bad things happen?"

I explained that bad things happen because there is sin in the world; that explanation held little comfort for her. As we continued to talk, the story came out. She was missing school because she was in court. Her uncle had been molesting her since she was five years old. The details were sketchy, but he had been arrested for another crime when he became a suspect in her molestation.

Grace was called to testify in court. However, that was not her biggest problem. Her grandmother, the mother of the uncle who molested her, became very angry at her for testifying against him in court. This completely crushed Grace. Although at a pivotal point in our conversation, the indifferent bell rang. Lunch was over. Back to the routine.

My mind was racing; how could this be? How many other students did I have, had, or would have with similar stories?

"Oh, Father God. How can I help?"

Grace came in from time to time after school to talk. We talked about love and how it could get so contorted that one could overlook the atrocity of another's behavior, thereby overlooking its horrible effects on an innocent person.

Grace was concerned about her relationship with her grandmother. Although very hurt, she came to realize that living in anger toward her grandmother would cause her much unhappiness. Grace asked me to pray for God to help her forgive her grandmother.

Time moved on. Grace graduated and went on to high school.

She came to visit me one day after school. She told me she was doing well, getting A's, and enjoying high school. Then she said, "I want to go to college and become a teacher. I want to be able to help other girls who have gone through what I have."

"I'm very proud of you!" I responded. "You are allowing God to use this very difficult experience for the good of others." We chatted a bit, hugged, and off she went.

As teachers, we often do not get to hear "the end of the story," but that does not diminish the blessings we receive from being part of the story.

"Do not be overcome by evil but overcome evil with good" (Romans 12:21 NIV).

~8~

JIMMY'S RESILIENCE

*J*immy was pleasant, hardworking, dependable, and a good student. As time went on, his attendance became irregular, causing his grades to drop. Once again, discipline was not the answer, but understanding was.

We had a talk, and he told me about his life. His father was in jail for shooting and killing his mother … Way past tragic, but there was more. Jimmy was present when his father shot his mother. As a result, he was now living with an aunt. Sadly, there was even more to this already tragic story.

He told me that a few weeks before, his aunt had told him to pack his clothes and get into the car. With no explanation, she brought him to a children's home, dropped him off, and left.

How did Jimmy deal with this?

He got some bus schedules and figured out which route would take him to school, which was about twenty miles from the children's home. He explained why his attendance had become sketchy; I listened in disbelief, anger, sympathy … How could I help him?

I referred him to the school counselor. Since it was just a few weeks before graduation, she arranged for Jimmy to stay at our school. She also arranged for his city bus transportation to be paid for by the district.

God's grace did not end there. The family of a friend of Jimmy's became aware of his situation and offered to have Jimmy stay with them. The court allowed them to become his guardians. Jimmy graduated and went on to high school. I have often wondered about him, but teachers don't always get to know the rest of the story. We feed into students for a time, and they continue swimming past us on their life's journey while we stay in place for others to enter our cove of teaching and caring.

~9~

... AND GIVE TONS OF THANKS TO GOD

I moved to a new school after being at one school for thirty years. Moving to a different school was a big change. Having been at the one for so long, I knew the staff and many of my student's families. Children of students I had years before were sitting in their parents' seats. When I realized that one of my students was a grandchild of a student who had been in my class, I really felt old!

The move helped me identify with students who moved a lot during their school years. I was now "the new kid on the block." As a result, I knew very little about the kids in my class and their families.

The first year at my new school, there were twin girls in my class. They were excellent students, bright and creative, and they always went above and beyond on projects and other assignments; just pleasant gals to be around. They were liked and respected by their peers; the perfect balance of preparing for their future while enjoying the present.

When parent-teacher conferences arrived after the first trimester, the twins came in with an older man, at least in his seventies. His appearance showed that he had been a hard worker, and his work clothes showed that he still was. He was clearly uncomfortable being there at school, but his concern for the girls was also clear. The girls were straight "A" students, so it was an easy conference. They told me that "John" was their grandpa, and they lived with him. Great, next conference … But I was curious about the rest of their story.

A few days later, I was talking with the girls during a break. I asked them if I could ask a few questions about them living with their grandparents. They said fine but clarified they didn't live with their grandparents, just their grandpa. So, a seventy-plus-year-old grandpa was raising twin granddaughters, alone.

This is the story they shared with me: Dad and Mom never married. They knew who their dad was, but he was never a part of their lives. They lived with their mom at her mother's and stepfather's house. A few years before, their mother was kicked out of the house. They didn't volunteer details, and I didn't ask. So now we have the twins living with grandma and step-grandpa … until grandma leaves. Again, no details. So, for the last year, they had been living with their step-grandfather.

Amazing! I told them I was proud of them for doing so well under these difficult circumstances. Their answer, expressed by the more outgoing twin, blew me away even more.

She smiled and said, "God gave us each other because He knew it would be tough. But we're together and we're fine. We make dinner for Grandpa; he works really hard and is tired when he gets home. We keep the house clean and do well in school so he doesn't have to worry about us." (This answer is paraphrased.)

And I think I have problems!

LANGUAGE ARTS AND SKILLS

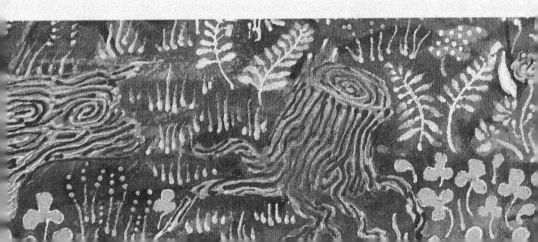

LANGUAGE ARTS AND SKILLS

*T*he fourth strand of our tapestry weaves a strong background color, allowing the other strands to stand out. This strand steadily teaches the arts and skills of language. Notice I have used both terms: art and skills.

Art implies beauty, and skill implies knowledge. Notice the conjunction "and." These concepts complement one another; they do not compete. They enhance one another; they do not exclude.

Think of the artist and the expert. While one may at first appeal to the heart and the other to the mind, our hearts and minds do not act independently or exclusively of one another. Whether these accomplishments are personal or historical, they are always a combination of heart, soul, and mind.

As we look at some of these arts and skills in the classroom, note how they entwine in our classroom tapestry.

1. WHY DIDN'T THEY TEACH ME THAT?

2. EXPOSITORY TEXT STRUCTURE PRACTICE

3. THE BIG PICTURE

4. 6+1 TRAITS OF WRITING

5. LEARNING HISTORY THROUGH ROCK AND ROLL

6. CULTURE

~1~

WHY DIDN'T THEY TEACH ME THAT?

"Why did you fail your science test? Didn't you read the book?" Mom asks accusingly.

"I *did* read it! I didn't understand it!" Johnny answers honestly. And the tension builds … Sound familiar?

Early in my career, I joined the Great Valley Writing Project. I learned more from that project than any other training I ever had. It not only helped me as a teacher but also as a learner.

I had been through the California teaching credential program, had a master's degree, and had been teaching for six years. What I learned at the GVWP conference, I had never heard before, at least not in that way. It wasn't really new information. Rather, it was a way to recategorize knowledge I already had.

As excited as I was, I was also angry. How had I been able to go through all that training to become a teacher and not been taught this? Why hadn't my high school or even elementary school teachers taught me this?

Teaching kids to read was obviously a very important part of my job. At the time, I was teaching fifth grade in a self-contained classroom. That meant I was teaching the same group of kids in all the basic subject areas—science, social studies, language arts, and math. I observed that reading in content areas, like science and history, was much more difficult for my students than reading a short story.

There are many reasons for that, the main one being student interest. OK. I got that. But just because they weren't interested didn't mean they didn't have to learn it. So, what could I do to help them become better readers in areas they had little interest in? I really struggled with that. Then, at this conference, I learned the secret!

Not all reading is equal!

Different reading techniques are required for different reading structures. What? Reading is reading … isn't it? Yes and no. The structure of texts differs according to its content's purpose.

How many of you know that the structure of most writing falls into two categories? Do you know what the categories are? Do you know what the structures are?

These are patterns of thought that should be encouraged at a very young age. Later, when I was teaching seventh and eighth grade, I used picture books to teach the text structure concept.

The first category is expository. Expository writing exposes, uncovers, or explains. It is typically used in content textbooks such as science, history, chemistry, physics, etc. There are many different structures of expository writing, which makes it more difficult to read. Learning the structures and how to recognize them improved my student's reading comprehension immeasurably. I saw many, many students move from being reading haters to reading lovers.

Just as a contractor can build more efficiently and effectively when they know how to read the blueprints for a building's structure, a reader can learn more efficiently and effectively by knowing the blueprint of the text's structure.

Following is a list of text structures (blueprints) commonly found in textbooks. It is not exhaustive and not exclusive to only mature readers. Notice the questions posed are for young children.

- Compare-Contrast Structure—examines the similarities and differences between two or more people, events, concepts, ideas, etc.

  How is a kitty like a puppy? (compare)

  How is a kitty different than a puppy? (contrast)

- Cause-Effect Structure—examines the causal relationship between a specific event, idea, or concept, and the results that follow.

  If you tell a lie (cause), what happens (effect)?

- Sequence—information is given in a specific order.

  How do you build a snowman? First, second, next…

- Chronological—information is given following the order of time.

  Make a timeline of the birthdays in your family (chronological).

- Problem-solution—the writing sets up a problem or problems, explains the solution, and then discusses the solution's possible effects.

  How can you solve the problem of your messy room?

- Descriptive—information given with the purpose of creating a visual or mental picture.

  Tell me about the colors and shapes in the picture that you drew.

  The other reading category is narrative. A narrative tells a story. Unlike the expository category, a narrative has one basic structure that will always have the following components:

- Characters—who is in the story
- Setting—time and place of the story
- Plot—conflict
- Moral—lesson

Narrative writing is easier to read. We all live narrative lives. We are all stories and have stories to tell. We are characters who live in a certain time and location. We all have conflicts, which cause problems in our lives. We learn lessons from dealing with the problems; not always good lessons, but we always learn something. It is called "experience."

Let's look at an example. After reading or telling the story of "Little Red Riding Hood," a child as early as two years old could be asked the following questions.

- Characters: Who is in the story? *Little Red Riding Hood, Big Bad Wolf, Grandma, Woodcutter*
- Setting (place): Where are they? *In the forest and at Grandma's house*
- Setting (time): When did the story happen? *Once upon a time …*
- Plot: What is the problem? *The wolf wants the basket of food that Little Red Riding Hood is bringing to her grandma, and she doesn't want to give it to him.*
- Moral: What did you learn? *Don't talk to strangers … don't walk away by yourself …*

Helping young children discover this basic narrative structure in the first stories they hear/read will help them when they tell/write their own stories. As they move into more complex stories with multiple story lines, identifying these pieces makes comprehension and retention much easier.

~2~

EXPOSITORY TEXT STRUCTURE PRACTICE

*A*s we were reading expository writings, I would ask my students to identify the text structure of various parts of the reading. I found this improved comprehension. I also found worksheets that had passages with the different structures, and we would build graphic organizers, visual shapes and patterns, showing the layout of the information.

Once students could see the structures showing the relationship of ideas in what they read, they used these structures as prewriting tools to write expository reports.

Another writing practice I used was to take an ordinary sentence, such as "My family is eating dinner," and restructure it into the various expository structures. For example:

Compare-Contrast Structure—examines the similarities and differences between two or more people, events, concepts, ideas, etc.

"My family is enjoying the meal prepared by my dad, except my little brother is spitting out his vegetables."

Cause-Effect Structure—presents the causal relationship between a specific event, idea, or concept and the events, ideas, or concepts that follow.

"When my little brother started spitting out his vegetables, we all started laughing."

Chronological Structure—gives readers a chronological order of events or a list of steps in a procedure.

"First, we cleaned things up, then we got dessert, then we took our showers and headed for bed."

Problem-Solution Structure—This type of structure sets up a problem or problems, explains the solution, and then discusses the effects of the solution.

"The problem my little brother caused will hopefully be resolved by him being told that if he does that again, he will not get dessert for the next week. That may solve it or it may cause other problems."

Descriptive Structure—This type of text structure features a detailed description to give the reader a mental picture.

"The spat-out green and yellow vegetables decorated the tablecloth and left an unpleasant smell that soured everyone's desire to finish their own dinner."

~3~

THE BIG PICTURE

Literacy is balancing the tension between meaning—what do I want to say—and structure—how do I say it.

Examining the layering of language is a very helpful exercise:

1. Words are the basic layer when we read, write, speak, or listen.

2. Words are joined with other words to form a specific meaning in a sentence.

3. Sentences are grouped together by commonality of meaning into paragraphs.

4. Paragraphs are joined to become various types of literary works.

Hanging in my classroom was a chart called "The Big Picture." As we were studying different levels of language, we would look at "The Big Picture" to identify the components of the level we were studying. For instance, if we were learning spelling and vocabulary, we would look under "Word" and see that we were dealing with spelling (structure) and vocabulary (meaning).

To help explain this, let me introduce a metaphor. It is important to teach with both a telescopic and a microscopic perspective. I'm sure most of you have worked on jigsaw puzzles. After dumping out the individual pieces on the table (microscopic view), you look at the big picture on the cover of the box (telescopic view). Seeing this "big picture" guides you as you put the pieces together to recreate the "big picture." Think of how many times you look at that "big picture" as you try to put the pieces together.

Imagine how difficult the puzzle would be if you did not have the "big picture" to check. Yet this is exactly what we do to students. We throw lots of details, puzzle pieces, and facts at them, but we never share what the big picture looks like.

THE BIG PICTURE

Word

Meaning - What do I want to say?

- vocabulary/semantics
- connotation/denotation
- synonym/antonym

Structure - How do I want to say it?

- beginning, middle, end
- root/base
- prefix/suffix
- syllables

Sentence

Meaning - What do I want to say?

- declarative
- interrogative
- imperative
- exclamatory

Structure - How do I want to say it?

- simple sentence
- compound
- complex
- compound/complex
- syntax – word order
- grammar – follow the rules

Paragraph

Meaning -What do I want to say?

- topic sentence
- supporting ideas
- further description
- concluding sentence

Structure - How do I want to say it?

- text structure
- mechanics
- indent
- dialogue
- capitals
- transitions
- coherence

Literary Work

Meaning - What do I want to say?

- descriptive
- narrative
- expository
- persuasive

Structure - How do I want to say it?

- reports
- book
- story
- poetry

~4~

6+1 TRAITS OF WRITING

I remember reading a comedy sketch performed by Jerry Seinfeld. It was about answering essay questions and getting a response from his teacher. Jerry's suggestion was to write everything you know about the essay question's topic and hope you came close to the correct answer. The response from his teacher was that his answer was "vague." He'd respond back to the teacher, "unclear," and back and forth they went …

As I was reading it, I completely identified with the frustration of both the student and the teacher.

In 1980, a group of teachers from around the country were asked to evaluate papers of all grade levels and identify the specifics of good writing. From this, six traits were identified as being evident in quality writing. Later, a seventh trait was added.

Yay! If they were identifiable, I could teach them to my students (and, of course, myself). No more bland "rewrite" or "needs improvement" phrases at the top of my student's work.

Let's look briefly at these 6+1 traits:

- Ideas—Start with great ideas that are clear and focused.
- Organization—Arrange these ideas in a way that is easy for readers to understand them.
- Voice—Show your unique personality in your writing.
- Word Choice—Use words that create images and emotions in your reader.
- Sentence Fluency—Vary sentence beginnings, lengths, structures, and rhythms.
- Conventions—Follow the rules of written language.
- Presentation (added later)—The initial look at the assignment sets a positive or negative attitude about the paper.

I would give students bad examples of one of the traits and ask them to rewrite and improve the example.

For instance: "The boy hit the ball thrown by the pitcher." Improve word choice.

"The skinny little boy at bat rocketed the fireball that was hurled by the pitcher and scored a home run."

Many benefits followed after using the 6+1 traits concept. First, we now had a common language that allowed us to communicate specifically about the varied aspects of writing. Now, instead of "rewrite" on top of their assignments, I would write, "Improve sentence fluency in the third paragraph" or "Work on clarifying the ideas."

Students also responded and edited one another's writing using the language of the 6+1 traits, and made suggestions to their classmates. This added to their own inventory of what was good and poor writing.

One unexpected result was that my student's reading comprehension noticeably improved. These writing traits became so familiar to them that in discussions, I would hear comments like, "I really liked the word choice and sentence fluency that Jack London used to describe summer changing into winter in *Call of the Wild*."

Now that warms a teacher's heart!

~5~

LEARNING HISTORY THROUGH ROCK AND ROLL

*O*ne project I did in an elective class was a combination of fun, entertainment, and education, much to the surprise of my students. I selected two rock 'n roll songs whose lyrics were about historical events. This was the middle 2000s when hip hop and metalcore were what the kids were listening to. They were not very excited about having to listen to rock 'n roll.

The first song was Billy Joel's "We Didn't Start the Fire." The lyrics point out that the current state of the world is not the fault of the current generation starting "the fire," but rather it is the cumulative effect of fires that have been burning since the beginning of time. Joel cites an eclectic group of events and people throughout history in the song.

Bob Dylan's song "With God on Our Side" was the next song we listened to. It recalls some questionable policies that the United States enforced, believing that God was on the country's side. The final event of the lyrics leaves the listener pondering the question, "Did Judas Iscariot have God on his side?"

Each student was to choose five events to research and write a short explanation about, which they would share in front of the class.

This elective required the students to engage in several activities that many of them did not like: studying history, research, presenting to the class, and listening to music they were convinced was old and boring. Doing them in the context of these songs, however, resulted in them having fun and being entertained and educated.

The proof was in the pudding when we were having some quiet free time. During this time, I would have soft music in the background. They knew I would not play their metalcore, but they asked if I would play some more rock 'n roll songs.

Elvis Presley and the Beatles, here we come!

~6~

CULTURE

*T*eaching both history and language arts in junior high required that we frequently talked about culture. It was a word the students understood vaguely but not specifically.

I did some research and came up with the acronym "AMERICA." The categories helped remove the vagueness of the word *culture* and specified what it covers. It can be used with a variety of cultural groups, including age groups, religious groups, political groups, level-of-education groups, etc.

AUTHORITY	Who is in charge?
MORAL	What is the standard for right and wrong?
ECONOMIC	Who produces and distributes wealth?
RELIGION	What do we believe?
INTELLECT	What knowledge do we value?
CUSTOMS	What traditions and holidays do we recognize?
ARTS	What do we admire as beauty?

It was a great tool while teaching US history to eighth-grade students. Studying the many conflicts that led to the American Revolution, Civil War, and the World Wars and so on led to a deeper understanding when looking at them through the lens of AMERICA.

As we read novels, both fiction and nonfiction, familiarity with these various aspects of culture improved comprehension and made for great classroom discussions and debates.

The first assignment asked the students to explain the culture of their family. One of the answers I remember was from a student about "'Authority—who's in charge?" She said her parents thought they were in charge, but really, her little brother was the one who ruled.

That opened a discussion of how reality can be very different from formal definitions in many areas of life. It is important for all of us to realize that the official explanation of a concept may be very different from the reality of how it plays out.

WEAVE YOUR OWN THOUGHTS

WEAVE YOUR OWN THOUGHTS

WEAVE YOUR OWN THOUGHTS

CLASSROOM
TIPS AND BITS

CLASSROOM TIPS AND BITS

T he good news about teaching is that once a year, in May, you are completely finished, and once a year in August, you start a brand-new school year, which provides a fresh start. The bad news is that between August and May, you are never caught up. This next section will have some strands of yarn that will make the school year roll a little easier.

CLEAR EXPECTATIONS

Start the school year with clear expectations. Define what you expect from the students and what the students can expect from you. And that was exactly what I did with my students the first day of school. The students wrote about expectations. The first section was "What I expect from Ms. DeJong as a teacher;" the second section was "What Ms. DeJong can expect from me as a student."

I wanted to convey two main ideas. First, I wanted to clarify the roles we each had in this classroom relationship. The reason we found ourselves together was for the purpose of education. Everything else was secondary. I was not there to be their friend. I was their teacher, and they were my students. That did not mean we couldn't like each other and even have a good time, but there was a boundary separated by the roles we each had in the classroom: me—teacher; them—students.

I recognized this importance after having a few student teachers. By the time I started teaching junior high, I had already taught for eight years and was thirty-eight years old. This idea of roles was not an issue in my fourth-and-fifth-grade classrooms. When I moved to junior high, however, it became a problem, as some of the student teachers were only eight or nine years older than my students. They looked like they could sit in a desk and blend right in with the class.

Ironically, in one case, it was the student teacher who had blurred the boundaries between teacher and student. She had a party and invited some students who were in my class. Alcohol was available, and the student teacher offered it to the students. Interestingly, it was some of my students who told me about it. They clearly knew it was wrong, and they called their parents to come and get them.

The second main idea is the necessity for each student to clearly understand the way the business of education would be done in the classroom, from grades to missing assignments, and from homework turned in without a proper heading to making up assignments after an excused absence. The students were always involved in setting these guidelines. Although I had the final word, it was always interesting how fair and effective their suggestions were.

CLASSROOM RULES

I started the year with a discussion of what rules we should have in the classroom. The kids made the usual suggestions of "no talking," "pay attention," "always come to class prepared," "follow directions," "keep your hands and feet to yourself," and so on.

It always got pretty detailed, so I suggested, "Let's keep it simple. How about boiling it all down to just one rule?"

They looked a little puzzled, so I asked them, "Why are you here?"

"To get an education," they responded.

"And why am I here?"

"To give us an education."

"How about making that the rule? 'Don't do or say anything that will interrupt you from getting an education and me from giving you one.'"

We agreed that would cover anything that might come up and were very pleased with ourselves.

"Let the education begin!"

HOMEWORK

In any of my classes, there would always be students who didn't do their homework. Dealing with this could be frustrating. However, at times this was legitimate. This was my general policy for homework:

- For every ten assignments, one missing assignment would be excused.
- One additional missing assignment per trimester would be excused with a note signed by a parent.
- I did not accept late work—period.
- If a student was absent, they had the number of days they were absent to turn the work in. Frequently, however, if a student checked with me about a missing assignment due to illness, I often excused them. I found that makeup assignments often overloaded students when they were already behind.
- Student projects and reports did not fall into this category and were never excused.

I told the students these guidelines at the beginning of the year and reviewed them periodically. Of course, there were situations that needed to be handled on an individual basis, but as a rule, these guidelines worked well. The trick was to make sure everyone knew them. You might even give a homework assignment on the homework assignment guidelines!

NO NAME, NO DATE, NO CLASS PERIOD NUMBER

Some students did not put the correct heading on their paper. This was a real problem when I was teaching six classes of different students each day.

To help deal with this in a light, humorous way, I made a coffin out of a small box with a tomb-shaped sign in front of it that said,

"REST IN PEACE"
No Name,
What a Shame,
No Credit for Eternity

Students could check the box outside of class time within two days of the due date and "resurrect" their nameless paper by putting the proper heading on it for partial credit. Every two days, I threw out the "dead" papers. They were then "lost forever."

Handling it this way gave the kids a chance to "save" their assignment while putting the responsibility for the rescue on them.

FAT FRIDAY

Every Friday in the teacher's lounge, the teachers had "Fat Friday." Each grade level of teachers and aides took turns bringing in goodies on Fridays, and we'd all pig out. My room was just across from the teacher's lounge, and I'd often walk out with my mouth full, trying to swallow the last bite before entering the classroom. This did not go unnoticed by my students. They asked if they could have Fat Friday too.

That sounded good, but it also sounded like it could get out of hand. So, I told the kids that we could have "Fat Friday" if we came up with some boundaries that would allow "Fat Friday" to happen without disrupting class time.

First, the students needed to earn it. I taught six periods a day. Across the whiteboard, I wrote:

P-1   P-2   P-3   P-4   P-5   P-6

During the week, if there was any misbehavior, I put a check under that class period. At the end of the period each Thursday, if the class had three or more checkmarks, they could not have "Fat Friday." This quickly led to the students monitoring each other, telling each other to "be quiet or we can't have 'Fat Friday.'" It was always one of the first things a new student was briefed on by the students when joining the class. Also, during Fat Friday, students were not allowed to share food in class or disrupt class in any way. They could not bring drinks other than water. Leaving a mess would get them a check for next week.

It worked out great! I was always impressed with the fairness that kids had when contributing to setting up rules to make the class run smoothly.

And, of course, donations of Snickers to the teacher were always appreciated!

READ THE QUESTIONS FIRST

A tip I told my students was to always read the comprehension questions given at the end of a story before reading the story. This applied to all subject areas that had questions at the end of a reading section.

Reading with the purpose of confirming or contradicting the knowledge the students took to the story from the comprehension questions added to the students' level of interest, and it definitely increased comprehension of the story.

FINAL WORDS

Teaching is a special profession. The Bible is very clear about this:

"Not many of you should become teachers, my brothers and sisters, for you know that we who teach will be judged by a higher standard" (James 3:1).

Your heart, soul, and mind are out there and vulnerable every minute of the day. There will be great joy along with dismay and sadness. The classroom is the devil's target. That has never been more true than in this present time. Always remember:

"Ye are of God, little children, and have overcome them: because greater is He that is in you, than he that is in the world" (John 4:4).

Fight the good fight! We know God wins and where we will be for eternity. In the new earth, I'm sure there will be schools. Who knows? We may be fellow teachers!

May God bless you greatly!

WEAVE YOUR OWN THOUGHTS

WEAVE YOUR OWN THOUGHTS

WEAVE YOUR OWN THOUGHTS

ORDER INFORMATION

Additional copies of this book can be ordered
wherever Christian books are sold.

Printed in the USA
CPSIA information can be obtained
at www.ICGtesting.com
LVHW092328051024
792903LV00005B/573